This book contains a short collection of articles, reports and readers' letters taken from Salford newspapers which were in circulation during the reign of Queen Victoria and the early part of this century. It gives a lighthearted view of the people of Salford, their work, their play and their everyday life. At the same time it shows the terrible social conditions endured by many during this period.

Tony Sumner Frankland, 1982

Salfordian ***Tony Frankland*** *is the Assistant Local History Librarian at the Salford Local History Library, Peel Park, Salford. His previous booklets published by Salford Local History Society, of which he is Secretary, include "The Diary of Abraham Driver" and "Salford's Prison".*

ISBN 0 907511 15 5

THE LAMPLIGHTERS OF MANCHESTER

Alderman Bowker pre over a tea meeting of city. The chairman, gathering of the cor that the lamplighters indispensable to mo introduction of gas. seen in Manchester was a very wonderful thing. The lights extended as far as Altrincham and nearly to Oldham; they were lighted and extinguished every night as if by magic; and every lamp, although the number was so vast, was faultlessly clean. The lamplighters were a class of men than whom none in the employ of the town council were better conducted, and it was a rare circumstance to find one of them brought before the Watch Committee for any offence.

(Salford Weekly News 15th February 1862)

SALFORD BOARD OF GUARDIANS

The weekly meeting of the Board was held yesterday; Mr G Yorston in the chair.

RELIEF

Indoor: 36 persons had been admitted to the workhouse during the week, 22 discharged, and there had been 1 birth and 8 deaths. The total number in the house at the end of the week was 655 against 648 on the last day of the preceding week, and 615 in the corresponding week of last year. 191 vagrants had been relieved during the week. There were 110 imbeciles in the house, and 83 lunatics in the workhouse asylums. 68 boys and 65 girls were attending the workhouse school; 29 of the former and 9 of the latter receiving industrial training.

Outdoor: 2,259 persons had been relieved out of doors during the week at a cost of £162.8s, against 2,856 persons at a cost of £207.15s in the corresponding week of last year.

IMPROVEMENT IN THE TRAMP WARDS

The House Committee has recommended that the clerk should prepare specifications for the erection of 18 beds in the tramp wards, and two cupboards for holding rugs. They further recommended that two cast-iron baths should be purchased for the bathroom, similar to the two at present there. The Chairman, in reference to this matter, stated that the committee had thought it desirable to have three or four baths, instead of two, as at present. They would cost no more than £2.5s or so each, and, if provided, would do away with any excuse for using the same water twice. They were approved by the board.

(Salford Weekly News 9th June 1866)

****

Dedicated to Tom, Julie & Jim, the Devo Doves

****

Published by Neil Richardson, 88 Ringley Road, Stoneclough, Radcliffe, Manchester M26 9ET

****

SABBATH NUISANCE

To the Editor of the Salford Weekly News:-

Sir, Will you kindly allow me to take up a little space in your valuable paper. I have long been expecting someone to call public attention to a great nuisance, created by the selling of crumpets, watercress, onions, etc., in the public streets on a Sunday. I have rarely been so much annoyed as I was by this practice when having breakfast last Sunday morning, and I believe it is worse in the afternoon. I heard no less than five or six hawkers of these commodities shouting and hawking as though they did not care a pin for anybody. I sincerely hope that the "men in blue" will look more strictly after these nuisance creators, and that the authorities will put a stop to the cause of complaint. By giving publicity to these few lines you will greatly oblige -

Yours etc.
A lover of the Sabbath

(Salford Weekly News 16th April 1870)

THE POLICE AND THE BOY BATHERS

To the Editor of the Salford Weekly News:-

Sir, The other evening, some half dozen youths passed my house in a state of nudity, closely pursued by a policeman. On inquiring I found they had been bathing in the canal, when the policeman disturbed them. Now, sir, I think it is a great pity that the population of our courts and alleys cannot enjoy a good wash without having to trouble the policeman thus. True, we have baths in Salford, but the charge is more than the poor can pay; and I would suggest the building of baths near Peel Park, for the upper part of Salford and Pendleton, but I think it would be money well spent to have them in the park itself; and I would propose that a few acres of land be enclosed and an open bath be constructed that would accommodate a couple of hundred youths at a time, at a nominal charge, say of one halfpenny, and to this might be added a few private baths. And then in winter the open water could be lowered to a foot in depth, and when frozen over would be a good and safe skating ground and would thus give health and recreation in summer and winter, and would most likely be one means of reducing the death-rate.

Yours, etc.
Pro Bono Publico

(Salford Weekly News 23rd July 1870)

DRUNKEN CARTERS

To the Editor of the Salford Weekly News:-

Sir, Will you be kind enough to allow me through the medium of your valuable paper to call the attention of the colliery proprietors and all other owners of horses, to the desirability of erecting a good sized and convenient watering trough at the junction of Little Hulton and Bolton turnpike, at Irlams-o-th'-Height, where the drinking fountain now stands. Carters would then water their horses without being compelled to call at the public houses; and cattle and sheep driven along the road from the market could quench their thirst. If this were done we should have less drunken carters on the road. Carters by calling at public houses for water are lead into temptation and induced by others who chance to be there to get more beer than they intended. There would also be a great saving in horses. It is my opinion, where one horse is worn out with work, two are starved to death with standing exposed to bad weather at public house doors after fatigue and sweating. Considering the great number of horses travelling on the roads, the expenses would not be too much if all parties who supply the fountain with water would supply the trough. If not, it would not be much for the horse owners to give yearly a subscription towards defraying the expenses. I shall be glad to assist in this object, pecuniarily and otherwise, if the matter is taken up.

Edward Davies, Feb. 28th 1872

(Salford Weekly News 12th March 1872)

THE STREET TRAMWAYS QUESTION

(Letter to the Editor of the Salford Weekly News)

Sir, The tramways have already been tried in Salford and pronounced a failure by a majority of the inhabitants, I am astonished that our Corporation are again entertaining the subject. I think they might find something better to do than wasting money of the ratepayers by sending tramway deputations to distant parts of the country (pleasant excursions, no doubt, but entirely uncalled for). As I live in Chapel Street, I had the best opportunity of seeing the operation of the tramway, and I came to the following conclusions from the evidence of what I myself saw:- First, Tramways are very dangerous to all horses travelling on the road. Second, They are dangerous to all vehicles, omnibuses excepted. Third, Tramways give an unfair monopoly of the roadway to omnibuses. I have seen a great many horses thrown down by the tramway. Since the tram(lines) was taken up there have been far fewer accidents of this kind. I have conversed with many persons who have horses, and they all condemn the system of tramways as dangerous. The feeling among ratepayers is that our Corporation is too fond of change, and are too apt to try crude experiments at other people's expense.

William Binns, Chapel Street

(Salford Weekly News 6th September 1873)

STREET ARABS

Two boys, 11 years of age, were charged by the School Board for being refractory. Samuel Ashworth Turnbull, lived with his parents at 6 West Booth Street, Pendleton, and proved that he had been incorrigible for nearly five years. James Alfred Percival, who lived with his parents at 2 Park Street, had been in the habit of following the omnibuses along the street, tumbling in somersaults on the pavements, and begging alms from the passengers. -Both boys were ordered to be sent to an industrial school until they are 16 years of age.

(Salford Weekly News 13th December 1873)

PEEL PARK TOUTS

(Letter to the Editor of the Salford Weekly News)

Sir, Will you allow me, through the medium of your paper, to make an enquiry respecting the conduct of certain persons who frequent Peel Park. Is it possible that visitors to a place so benevolently thrown open to the public cannot be presented from annoyance when enjoying its pleasant walks? Must they continue pressing upon them the use of their cottages, with their doubtful accommodation; instead of the comfortably prepared refreshment always ready within the enclosure? So excitable and determined are some of these busy applicants, that many visitors have to hold their satchels and baskets with a firm hand, for if they can be secured, of course the owners must follow. For my own part, if this state of things must continue, I and my friends will have to give up seeking enjoyment where we are thus dogged at every turn in the walks. Hoping there will soon be a change in the state of things, I am

&c.

(Salford Weekly News 13th September 1873)

THE BASSINETTE EXQUISITE.

IN ALL SHADES CASH OR CREDIT.,

THE BEST OF THE SEASON.

Both in Quality and Price.

Fitted with Extra Thick Tyres.
Tubular Levers and Storm Aprons.
Nickel-plated. Adjustable Hood Joints.
Leather-lined Hood.
Tangent Spoke Wheels, etc.

CALL AND SEE THEM AT

PARKINSON BROS.,

219-223, CROSS LANE.

(Opposite the Palace).

ASSAULT UPON A KNOBSTICK CARTER

Samuel H-------, a carter in the employ of the Lancashire and Yorkshire Railway Co., was summoned for assaulting a carter in the employ of Messrs. Thomas McKay & Co., named William Bailey, during the late strike.

The prosecutor said that about four o'clock in the afternoon of Saturday the 19th instant, he was going down New Bailey Street with his horse and lurry. About 100 carters and 'nippers' who were on strike, were on the other side of the street. The 'nippers' began to hoot witness and call him a 'knobstick'. He (witness) put his horse in the stable and then came into the street where the men were standing. They again hooted him and he got hold of one of the 'nippers' and shook him. The defendant came up and said 'knock him down, he is nothing but a knobstick', and afterwards struck witness in the face, knocked him to the ground and kicked him. The defendant said that the complainant struck the 'nipper' several times in the face, and several witnesses were called to substantiate the fact. He admitted that he took the part of the lad.

Sir John Iles Mantell said that the complainant was no doubt agitated at being called a 'knobstick', and cuffed one of the 'nippers'. If the lad had been struck, there was the legal remedy for that, and the defendant did a great wrong to strike the complainant.

The defendant was fined 30s.

(Salford Weekly Chronicle May 31st 1873)

WORKHOUSE LUXURIES

(Letter to the Editor of the Salford Chronicle)

Sir, Considering the cost of Pauperism to the nation is now £12,000,000 yearly it is surely the duty of those in office to see that the poor-rate is economically applied. It is a notorious fact that the best class of working people have an even morbid terror of the 'house'. These are the elite of their class; and though reverses may occasionally bring them to the very margin of pauperism, they manage not only to keep off the rates themselves, but also to pay for the support of those persons more unfortunate, or, as is too often the case, less frugal and independent, who have become "chargeable to the parish". No one wishes to see the pauper deprived of any of the necessities of life, but it is certainly wrong to tax the hard-working and frugal ratepayer to supply him with luxuries. The supply of intoxicating liquors is in many workhouses a scandal, to which attention has often been called. A short time since the Salford Guardians advertised for contracts for provisions to be supplied during the present half-year. Amongst them are items which need some explanation. The cost of 321b of snuff S.P. and of 2001b of tobacco may not add very largely to the annual total cost of the Salford union, but it is surely unfair to spend any of the public money in supplying paupers with narcotics which all confess to be quite needless, which many think positively harmful, and which are admitted on all hands to be themselves fruitful sources of improvidence and want. I am, &c.

A Ratepayer

(Salford Chronicle 16th August 1873)

STRAY DOGS IN SALFORD

At the Borough Police Court on Wednesday, 19 persons were summoned and fined for permitting dogs to be at large and unmuzzled. An order for permitting dogs was issued by the Mayor on the 23rd June, and during the seven days of that month, 31 dogs were seized, by the police. During the present month 253 have been seized, and of the total number of 284, 36 have been claimed by the owners, making the total number destroyed since the 23rd June, 248.

(Salford Chronicle 2nd August 1873)

WANTED

by the Guardians of the Salford Union, a respectable female as Nurse, at the Workhouse hospitals, at a salary of £16 per annum, increasing to £18 and £20 per annum if the duties are satisfactorily performed, with board and lodging in the Workhouse, Eccles New-road, Salford, any week day between 3 and 5pm.

Appilcations stating age, enclosing testimonials, and endorsed "Nurse", must be sent to me, on or before Tuesday, the 22nd of July inst.

By order T H Bagshaw - Clerk to the Guardians, Union Offices, Eccles New-road, Salford 11th July 1873.

(Salford Chronicle 12 July 1873)

RATS

To insure freedom from these destructive and dangerous pests, use

"RODINE" RAT POISON

It makes a clean sweep in one night. Get a tin now.

[illegible] 2/8, 5/-. Post 3d. HARLEY, Chemist, Perth

Henry Tinker, Chemist, Pendleton,

Manchester.

C. W. Monk, Chemist,

193, TRAFFORD ROAD, SALFORD.

RIVAL TEETOTALLERS

To the Editor of the Salford Chronicle.

Sir, I hope you will allow me a small space in your valuable paper on a subject of importance to the inhabitants of Salford. I don't know whether you are aware of there being two meetings held on Sunday morning; -one by the Alliance, and the other terming themselves moral suasion teetotallers, - at Oldfield Lane, and of the animosity and vituperation carried on from this platform. On Sunday, the 28th inst., the proceedings opened with a short speech full of bitterness and hatred to workers in the same cause, but differing from them slightly in views, from the chairman (combined with extracts from Reynolds newspaper). After that came the speech of the day by a Mr Collins, and for vileness and scurrilous language I never heard the like. The sooner such scenes as this are put to a stop by the authorities the better. A great many working men were present, and everyone with whom I came in contact said the language was disgraceful. Some artizan among the crowd dissented from his views, and he was immediately asked to stand upon the platform. This he did, and denounced the conduct of the moral suasionists in most appropriate terms, and in a very sound speech, but Mr Collins was so outraged at opposition that he began his blasphemy, calling the man in the most frightful manner and because the meeting would not endorse his opinion he deliberately placed his thumb to his nose and extended his fingers. Then a tumult arose, and the meeting was stopped for some time, amidst cries of "He ought not to be allowed to address intelligent men". Now, sir, I would ask you if such scenes on a Sunday tend to the elevation of the working men, or whether they make teetotallers of them? What drunkard there could see a creditable example to follow? I believe one and all were completely disgusted. I should not have been surprised if such conduct had emanated from the taproom, but from a man professing philanthropy I am truly astonished. The sooner such proceedings are put to a stop the better, for I consider it a disgrace. Hoping to have your aid in removing this from our midst on the day of rest, I remain,

yours, AN OBSERVER

(Salford Weekly Chronicle 18th October 1873)

PAXMANS "AXLLL," KEYLESS WATCH 15/6.

The Finest Watch Value ever offered.

Thousands already running Highly-finished Jewelled Movement, Fine Gilt Plates, Hard Enamelled Dial, Sound and Reliable Keyless Work, Steel Hands, Excellent Timekeeper, Fully Warranted.

Solid Nickel Dust and Damp Proof Case.

15/6 post free. 2 for 30/-

PAXMAN & SONS,

WATCH FACTORS,

90/92, CROSS-LANE, SALFORD.

STEALING BOOTS FROM A WOMAN'S FEET

Edward Williams, labourer, Cook Street, Salford, was charged with stealing a pair of boots from Catherine Young, in the Royal Inn, Chapel Street. On the prisoner being taken into custody the boots were found concealed under his coat. On Wednesday the complainant and the prisoner, who have cohabited together for about four years, were drinking together, and the prisoner took the boots from the woman's feet, for the purpose of pawning them. The prisoner was committed for a month with hard labour.

(Salford Weekly Chronicle 2 August 1873)

THE SALFORD VOLUNTEERS AT ST PHILIP'S CHURCH

Sir, On Sunday last this celebrated Corps, consisting of 9 officers, 41 band, and 281 rank and file, honoured St Philip's Church by attending divine service, and, as usual, accompanied by a large crowd of the great unwashed, to the no small annoyance of the congregation and the inhabitants in the immediate vicinity. For fear that you should suppose that this number attended the service, permit me to say that upwards of 57 (including the sergeant-major and the band-sergeant or master) remained outside during the whole of the service, keeping in good humour their respective friends and followers by forming little groups, and thus reminding one of St Matthew's Church, Campfield, during Easter week. Thus assisted, the police (after being reinforced by additional officers), had no difficulty in keeping order, and restraining the crowd from becoming an intolerable nuisance. Surely sir, the time has now gone by when such a farce ought to be countenanced. If the parishoners of this or any other church kindly place at the disposal of this semi-military corps their parish church for the purpose of attending divine sevice, in justice, I maintain, they ought to be protected from such a want of consideration for their feelings as that of last Sunday, which, in my opinion, reflects little credit upon the officers for not taking the necessary precautions to avoid such a display. If this redoubtable Corps wish to impress the minds of the public with a sense of their military grandeur, let them conduct themselves in a becoming manner when attending a place of worship, and not make a farce of it by part only joining the service, and the remainder materially assisting, by their presence, the disorder of the crowd outside. In conclusion, allow me to add, that but for the 56th Lancashires we should have had at least one quiet Sunday, only 46 of the regular troops being present, which to their credit, be it said, entered the building and took their seats in a creditable manner, which example the Salford Corps will do well to imitate the next time they attend either this or any other church for divine service.

Yours, etc.,
AN OBSERVER

(Salford Weekly News 20 September 1873)

WOOD PAVING

The Improved Wood Pavement Company (London) having entered into a contract with the Corporation, are now laying down 500 yards of their pavement - blocks cut on end with the grain, and laid with asphalte joints on two crossed layers of planking - on Chapel Street, facing the Royal Dispensary. The principal advantages claimed for this mode of paving are perfect noislessness, great durability, facility of cleaning or sweeping, good foothold for horses, and great suitability for tramways.

(Salford Weekly News 22 March 1873)

THE SALFORD SUNDAY FOOT RACES

To the Editor of the Salford Weekly News,

Sir, An advertisement appeared in your last week's issue which commenced with the above heading. On reading the announcement I felt quite shocked, and more especially at the conclusive part, where "the aldermen and councillors of Salford are particularly requested to attend." I began to wonder whether it was intended to be a burlesque upon these gentlemen, or whether it was a hoax or a reality, or meant as an open defiance of law and order by the competitors and those who participate in the sports. However, to satisfy my mind, and in order to gain information on the subject, I ventured to go to the district indicated in the advertisement, "A meadow near to Ordsall Hall". I arrived upon the grounds at three o'clock, being half an hour earlier than the time mentioned. In forming an estimate as to the number of individuals upon the meadow, I should say there were about 500, whose ages varied from 10 to thirty years, but chiefly from sixteen to twentyfour. They were occupied in a variety of ways. The noise and animation were great. There were a great many dogs there, and of course many dog races; and what with the shouting of human beings and the yelping of the dogs, the noises were deafening. Many were engaged in jumping and wrestling. The greatest feature of the afternoon was "pitching and tossing"; I counted twelve groups at once eagerly bent on the game. I saw no foot races in the real sense of the term. I asked about them and was informed they had been contested in the morning. I was invited by a very keen sportsman to come next Sunday, as the sports would be unusually attractive - a very good programme - several handkerchiefs were to be run for, and some silver cups, and the sports were to conclude with a little boxing between members of the canine family and sundry gladitorial exercises between members of the human family. My sympathy warms towards the farmer, for it is a great trespass; the ground is much trodden, and where it ought to be green is brown. At the annual inspection of police, last week, Captain Terrers is reported to have said that "the Corporation has acted wisely in raising the force to 200 men". He spoke in very complimentary terms of some of his staff and said they were men of real intelligence and subtle intellect and of some as being able to "cope with the large criminal population with which we are surrounded". Can none of the above satellites devise some means to put a stop to such scenes as I have endeavoured to describe? How would it be to have a "battue" every now and then? I fancy if about fifty officers were to surround them and hem them well in on the land side - there would be many who would seek safety in flight, and not hesitate even to take to the water in the river Irwell where ford there is none; which, if it did nought else, might cool their ardour for Sunday sports. At all events, I should be delighted to see the police try what they could in this matter.

Yours, etc.,
HELTER SKELTER

(Salford Weekly News March 1874)

THE LOST GIRL FROM LOWER BROUGHTON

To the Editor of the Salford Weekly News:-

Sir, Some time has elapsed since you inserted in your paper an advertisement about the young girl Clara Whalley of Beech-street, Lower Broughton, who has been missing since the 31st August last. May I ask you to insert this note in your valuable paper. She left home on the morning of the above date, with the intention of going to her work in Pendleton, where she was employed as a weaver, but did not arrive at the place of her business. No reason is assigned for her absence, as she was on good terms with her parents and companions. She attended her Sunday School, and bore an excellent character for attendance and devotion. She is of good figure, low in stature, rather lusty, and has a full face; blue eyes, long auburn hair flowing to her back; and ruddy cheeks. She is just turned fourteen years of age. She was in her working attire when she left home; a black stuff dress, wearing clogs, white linen apron, scarlet and white handkerchief, puce coloured stockings, and dark drab-ground shawl, with white stripes. Any information on this subject is anxiously sought by her parents and friends, or by the Superintendant of Police, Town Hall, Salford. Should this communication attract the attention of daily or weekly papers, publicity of the above is earnestly desired by the missing girl's desponding parents and friends.

Yours, etc.,
RICHARD WHALLEY,
17 Beech-street, Lwr Broughton

(Salford Weekly Chronicle 20 November 1875)

THE OPENING OF THE MUSEUM, ETC., ON SUNDAYS

Sir, By this morning's newspapers I see that the Salford Town Council has refused to allow the picture gallery at the museum to be opened on Sundays. I think that this important decision will meet with the approval of every person who has a real desire for the true elevation of the people. Are we to break down, even for the sake of art, those deep feelings of reverence with which Englishmen and Scotchmen have been taught to regard the Sabbath day? What must be the consequence to religion, to morality, to philanthropy, and to everything of an elevating character, if such rash work as this is to be done? We are solemnly and expressly commanded to keep the day holy. Are we to trample down the divine command, and thus prepare the way for the worst evils? A disregard for this blessed day has perhaps brought on nations and individuals more calamity and ruin than anything else. Scores who have ended their days on the gallows began early in life by breaking the Sabbath; nations which have suffered the most awful calamities - cities which have been invaded, and perhaps destroyed, have been notorious for their wilful indifference to the sanctity of the Sabbath. Let the would-be openers of museums look round on the state of society. Let them pity the poor postmen, half deprived of their Sunday; the poor busmen, and their horses toiling away on Sundays as on weekdays; and let them look at the thousands engaged in the sale of liquors, to whom the Sunday is, for many hours, a day of toil. and let us try to secure rest and right for these, instead of outraging the consciences of men by proposing to open secular places on Sunday. I trust we shall hear no more proposals to open the Salford Museum on Sundays.

I am, etc., A HAPPY FIRESIDE

(Salford Weekly Chronicle 12 August 1876

SALFORD GAS v CANDLES

To the Editor of the Salford Weekly News:-

Sir, In allowing me the medium of your paper to call the attention of the Salford Gas Committee and "those whom it may concern" to the miserably defective supply and quality of gas which consumers have had to put up with during the past week, I believe you will confer a public benefit. Night after night, but notably Tuesday and Wednesday last, both in the streets and in our dwellings, the gas might be compared to "farthing" rushlights, just rendering darkness visible. In my own house, although we use large burners, candles had to be lighted, which in point of simile seemed to "snuff out" the gas. At an hotel close by, and which for the sake of furnishing the authorities proof, I will name (Mr. Madeley's Railway Hotel, Cross Lane), candles had to be brought in to supplement the gas. Now, sir, I think it is a shame, considering the high price we pay for gas in Salford, that we cannot get a good article, and plenty of it too, especially at this time of the year. Surely labour is not so scarce that the supply cannot be met, nor can coal be deficient. Whatever the cause may be, I trust the Gas Committee of managers will afford some explanation of the same and promise that the grievances shall not occur again.

Yours etc., BETTER LIGHT
Regent Road, Salford. August 26th

(Salford Weekly News 28 August 1875)

THE POLICE FORCE

To the Editor of the Salford Weekly News:-

Sir, A most painful feeling must enter the minds of the various members of the Salford Police Force when they read the statement made at a recent meeting of the Borough Council, that sixty percent of them had been convicted of drunkenness. A more alarming statement could not be made, taking into consideration the important duties they have to perform. No doubt the explanation afterwards given considerably toned down the announcement but still the fact remains that drunkenness has prevailed to a considerable extent among the members of our police force. It therefore becomes the duty of every constable to try and redeem not only his own character, but that of the force to which he belongs, and to acquire once more the goodwill of the inhabitants of this important Borough.

In dealing with this question it may be asked, have the proper means been taken to put a stop to this evil? On this point it is only just to say that the Chief Constable has from time to time spoken to and advised the men to lead a sober and upright life, plainly pointing to the advantages sure to result therefrom. Punishments have been severe enough; fines, stoppages of leave, and dismissals have been without end, but still the evil goes on without abatement. If that be so, why not try some other plan? Why not at once introduce a system of badges or stripes; as a reward for good conduct, accompanied by some little extra pay - a thing at present unknown in the Salford Police? Let some distinguishing mark be placed upon men of good character, so that the public may know them from others. Oft times do men of unblemished character deplore that they must bear the odium which falls to their share for no unworthy act of their own. If men in possession of these good conduct badges or stripes disgrace themselves, then deprive them of their distinguishing mark for a long time, and thus degrade them in the eyes of the public. This would be a far more terrible punishment than any amount of fines or stoppages of leave that might be levied on them.

I am sure that the people of Salford would never begrudge the little extra expense the system might entail, so long as it brought about a beneficial result, which, without doubt it would; and soon transform the Salford Police into an excellent body of men, of whom the Chief Constable,the Watch Committee, and the people of Salford might feel justly proud.

Yours, etc.,

(Salford Weekly News 31 March 1877)

DANGEROUS FREAK OF A DRUNKEN MAN

Yesterday afternoon, at half past 3 o'clock, a man named Edward Heeney, joiner, Barlow Street, Salford, climbed upon the parapet of Victoria Bridge and jumped into the water, a distance of over 10 yards, alighting on his feet. The water was only about three feet deep, and he was able to walk up the river bank, with the apparent intention of again entering the water, but some men who had witnessed the affair followed him and gave him into custody. Heeney was in liquor at the time, but when taken to the Police Station did not seem much the worse for his adventure.

(Salford Weekly Chronicle 14 July 1877)

PUBLIC BATHS AND WASH HOUSES, WHERE SHALL THEY BE PLACED?

Dear Sir, With your permission I should like to make a suggestion through your columns. It appears that the Town Council have at last decided that a certain sum be expended in providing baths and wash houses for the borough of Salford, and as some of the council object to so much money being spent for this purpose, I would suggest that the baths be erected in the parks (if it is legal). It would save considerable expense in the purchase of land, and one in Peel Park, I know, would be very acceptable and convenient to a large population. If a swimming bath were made for boys only, say under 16 years of age, and they were allowed its use for a small fee, I think it would be a blessing to the rising generations, as many boys are very anxious for a bathe, and parents also would not feel the same objections to their children bathing in a place of cleanliness and safety. I think it is quite possible to make the baths in the parks of even more use, by having a balcony round the room inside over the warm baths, so that plants usually stored in greenhouses during the winter months might be there deposited in case of need, and preserved by being kept at a fair temperature with the waste heat of the bath-room. Hoping something will be done in providing the much-needed baths, I remain yours, etc.,

E.R.

(Salford Weekly Chronicle 14 July 1877)

TREES IN TOWNS

To the Editor of the Salford Chronicle:-

Sir, We have had several leaders and letters in the paper lately about the planting of trees in towns. Among the suitable places named was the terrace between the rails and the river in front of the Crescent, Salford, and extending from near the Dispensary to Peel Park gates. I remember that bank being well covered with trees and shrubs, chiefly the willow kind, however - which I suppose got it the name of the "Willow Bank" -- but all the trees of whatever kind were of a fine healthy character. The foliage, in summer, was so full that it was no difficult matter to hide in any part of it. I think there must be some still living in Salford who may remember this as well as I do, and also the cause of its destruction - namely, the great crowd of people who came to see a grand aquatic tournament which took place on that part of the river Irwell which winds round the foot of that terrace. It may be noted that the Irwell had not so bad a character for mud and filth as it has since acquired, and at the point named was a considerable depth, at least I should think 6ft. I can also say that I have caught fish, and have eaten pie made of eels caught on lines baited with worms, out of the length between Peel Park and Castle Irwell. I understood at the time that the said tournament was got up and carried out by the officers of the regiments then stationed in Manchester and Salford; but for what purpose, or the exact date when it took place. I have no means of knowing except memory, which intimates the summer of 1824 or 1825 as likely to be the time. I write entirely from my own reflection and observation of the spectacle, which I will try to describe. In the field enclosed by the loop of the river two tents were erected at opposite sides of the ground, fitted up with suitable accommodation where the men could retire and change their clothes, and also get refreshment. The band of the regiment was present, the drummers taking a prominent part in the proceedings. Those who took part in the tournament were dressed in special uniform, and had the appearance of our modern cricketers when at play. On the river were placed two row-boats, with oarsmen and coxwain, one for each side. These boats were fitted up with a small platform, which projected about two feet over the bow of the boat, and was about 1ft wide. On this small stage the men had to stand when going into action. The man on each boat was provided with a pole 8ft or 9ft long, padded at both ends, and decorated with coloured streamers. These were the weapons of offence and defence. A stake was fixed in the river at each end to represent the starting point of each boat. When everything was ready, the signal was given for battle by the drummers sounding a regular "Tattoo", when each boat would glide off steadily to meet its antagonist about midway between the two starting points. Then commenced the tug of war. Each chevalier would try to plant the end of his pole against the breast of his adversary, and push him off his little stage into the river with a splash, amid the shouts and glee of all the beholders. The swimming then began, each getting out and retiring to his respective tent, amid the applause of his friends to dress. The result of it all was the almost entire destruction of the trees, the old Willow Bank being left a complete wreck. We wanted then our vigilant corporation, who, I think, would not have allowed such a thing to take place; yet I believe we were all trespassers, but then it must be remembered that the police force of the borough was very limited at that time, and the tresspassers very numerous.

Yours, etc., J HULME

(Salford Weekly Chronicle 10 August 1878)

J. H. & W. G. LOFT,

Adaptors and Extractors

OF

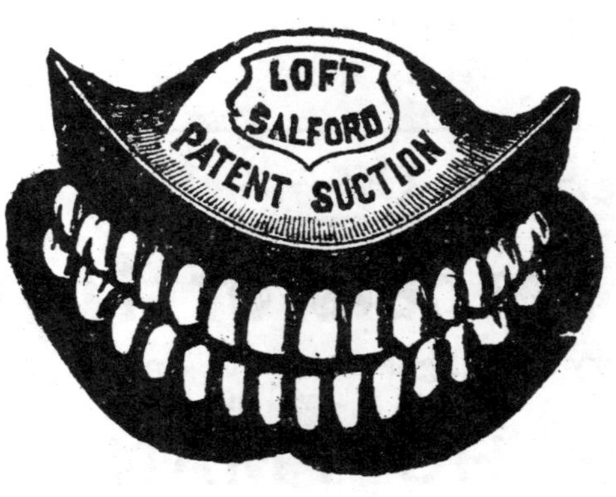

SET, UPPER OR LOWER, FROM 30/-
SINGLE TOOTH FROM 2/6.

Fit, Workmanship, Appearance, and Utility Guaranteed.

273, REGENT RD., SALFORD.

OUTRAGEOUS CONDUCT IN BLACKFRIARS STREET

To the Editor of the Salford Chronicle:-

Sir, When the corporation made New Blackfriars Street, if they had done their duty to the public they would have enclosed the waste land. Why should the land in Frederick Street, Pendleton - a quiet street - be advertised for enclosure, and the land in Blackfriars Street - cutting in two a neighbourhood infested with thieves and prostitutes - be unenclosed? All through the day, and especially on Sunday, the roughs amuse themselves as follows - whiptop, duckstone, kite flying, cricket, football, pigeon flying, pitch and toss, and stone throwing. £5 8s is what I shall have paid when the two windows now broken are put in - over 2s a week for the last 12 months - a tax put upon me that I never bargained for. Do the Watch Committee know that the police have, for three years, systematically neglected this street, and by their regulated absence made this road difficult to pass along during the day, and positively dangerous at night? Do the Watch Committee know that the police have had a "set" on this street ever since it was made, and their determination not to "man" it has lasted to the present moment. If an officer is put on one day a week, a month or three months, may pass before another appears. The man selected looks like a new hand, and not at all fit to grapple with the roughs who swarm out of the side slums, like bees, and take possession of the flags and unenclosed plots. How much longer will the corporation, for the sake of a few pounds, allow this open land to be used as a place of convenience from and out of Chapel Street? Is it to be enclosed? One young girl has been killed by stone throwing, the jury returning a verdict that the deceased was killed by a stone, but there is not sufficient credence to show by whom the stone was thrown. Not a week passes but some boy or girl is robbed of a parcel or an umbrella. On Saturday night last a young female had her ear rings snatched out of her ears, and on Sunday night about 10.30 I was closing my premises when two men came across the street from the vacant lot opposite, and with a blow of some sort of weapon felled me to the ground, splitting my head open for two inches. They were prevented from robbing and further ill-treating me by two young men who came up and gave chase to my assailants, who ran across to the dark entry right opposite my door and there they stood at bay. Not daring to go near, the young men came back and so it has been with all the assailants in this street, a hop, skip, and a jump takes them out of reach of the law. 50,000 people at the very least use this road in a week. Will the Corporation enclose this land for PRO BON PUBLICO.

(Salford Weekly News 15 March 1879)

BATHS EXHIBITION

Sir, I wish, with your permission, to record my indignation and disgust at the indecent exhibition which, under the title of "Swimming Gala", was provided by the Baths Committee of the Corporation at the opening of the new baths in Blackfriars-street on Wednesday evening last. Great stalwart men, in an almost complete state of nudity, were paraded before a mixed company of ladies, gentlemen and children with a shameless affrontery. The clothing they had on was so imperceptible as to make the term "pair of drawers" quite ridiculous. A savage, untutored Zulu would have been ashamed to appear before civilized society so stark naked as these men appeared. I unhesitatingly say that if any printseller undertook to publish photographs of these swimmers in the state they appeared before the company on Wednesday evening, a prosecution for selling obscene photographs would be instituted by the police. That there was no necessity, so far as the competition was concerned, for these men to appear so destitute of dress is proved by the fact that one man (with more modesty and sense than his fellows) competed in a light full-length costume, and won his race with ease. Of course I shall be twitted with prudery in making these remarks but I feel sure that the very members of the committee who arranged (thoughtlessly) this indecent exhibition will upon calm reflection admit that they should have restricted the spectators to gentlemen or insisted in all competitors dressing in a proper bathing costume.

Yours, etc., OLD FASHIONED MODESTY

(Salford Weekly News 12 June 1880)

A TRAM SERVANT

Sir, Would you allow me through the medium of your valuable paper to call the attention of the Manchester and Salford Tramways Company to their servant at the junction of Chapel Street and Oldfield Road. I have seen him on many a stormy day attending to his duty at the points for working traffic for Pendleton, Eccles and Patricroft, half-starved and no doubt wet to the skin, eating his scanty meal in the public street. I would like to ask, Are the Company too poor to provide shelter for their servant? His hours are from 8.30am to 10pm - too long to stand in the street this weather. I do not see why he could not have a hut, also a lever to work underground from the hut, same as on the railway. Hoping something will be done on his behalf, I remain,

Yours, etc.,
A LOVER OF HUMANITY

(Salford Weekly Chronicle 1881)

LEWD WOMEN IN CROSS LANE

Sir, Anyone passing through the above street between the hours of 9 and 11 at night must be surprised at the great number of loose women with which this street and neighbourhood abound, notwithstanding the fact that there is a police station established there. I think this matter calls for more vigilance. One cannot walk along without being accosted by these persons. It is also quite unsafe for any respectable female to walk down the lane, as serious cases of assault have already taken place.

Yours, etc.,
DECENCY

(Salford Weekly Chronicle 17 June 1882)

Great Sale of PIANOS & ORGANS.

New and Second-hand, by all the Best Makers,
Many Pounds below other people's prices.

PIANOS from 10 - Monthly. ORGANS 6 - Monthly.

Guaranteed 10 years and delivered free any distance on first deposit, and in case of sickness or bad trade, payment is not expected.
Old Pianos taken in exchange and good value allowed.
Railway Expenses allowed to Customers
Note our Name and Address.—
KENNA-SMITH,
116, Regent Road, Salford, corner of Oldfield Road,
OPEN EVERY DAY AND NIGHT TILL 11 O'CLOCK; SATURDAYS ALSO.

SPECIAL PRAYER FOR SUNDAY CLOSING IN ENGLAND

To the Editor of the Salford Chronicle:-

Sir, Kindly permit us to earnestly ask your many readers to devote a period between February 11 and 18 to thanksgiving for the blessing which has attended the efforts to stop the sale of intoxicating liquors on Sunday, and to specially pray that our Heavenly Father may graciously guide and bless the attempts to carry the bill for England this coming session of parliament.

Yours, etc.,

ROBERT WHITWORTH
T.A.STOWELL M.A.
EDWARD WHITWELL

(Salford Weekly Chronicle 10 February 1883)

AS EASY AS EASY
Our Furniture
AND

OUR
Payment System
Howarth & Co.,
LATE E. DOBB
105 & 107 Broad St.,
PENDLETON.
Ask to see our No. 1 SUITE.

OLD TRAFFORD POLICE SOUP KITCHEN

To the Editor of the Salford Chronicle:-

Sir, With your permission, I desire through your columns to tender my grateful acknowledgements to the large number of friends in various parts of the country who have so kindly forwarded me contributions in aid of the Old Trafford Soup Kitchen. Owing to the number and liberality of the contributions I have now, I am happy to say, sufficient funds in hand to carry on the work throughout the remainder of the winter. It will probably be interesting to the subscribers to know that up to the present about 40,000 hot suppers have been supplied, and the number of persons at present attending nightly, the vast majority of whom are children of tender years, average about 1,400. I have also been enabled to distribute to the most necessitous upwards of 200 pairs of clogs, together with other articles of suitable clothing, all of which are stamped with the Old Trafford Police mark. In closing, I would take this opportunity of thanking the police officers who each evening so willingly devote a large portion of their leisure time to the preparation and distribution of the suppers, and without whose aid it would be impossible for me to carry on the operation of the soup kitchen.

Yours, etc., JAMES BENT
SUPERINTENDANT,
County Police Office,
Old Trafford, Manchester

(Salford Weekly Chronicle 20 January 1883)

WEASTE TRAMCARS

To the Editor of the Salford Chronicle:-

Sir, Can any of your readers inform me whether the Carriage Company have power to lay tram lines anywhere they like? I have a large coal-yard and stabling in Heyworth street, adjoining the entrance to the Weaste car shed. The other week the pavers commenced taking up the street, and to my astonishment, have laid lines all along the same as a siding for their cars. These they have laid past the entrance gate of my yard, which is a great nuisance and inconvenience. Having some conveyances stabling here, I consider it will be an injury to me, as it is both awkward and dangerous turning in and out of the yard, they have left bare room for a conveyance to pass on one side only. There are often as many as five cars on the siding at once. I shall be glad to know if there is any remedy for the above.

Yours, etc., R OWEN,
129 Bridson Street, Weaste.

(Salford Weekly Chronicle 29 August 1885)

For Falling Hair, Scurf, or Dandruff, and Premature Baldness (Alopicia), USE

Krinks' "Never Fall,"

REGD.

The Guaranteed Cure or money returned.

W. J. KRINKS,

Hairdresser and Consulting Hair Specialist,

61, BROAD STREET, PENDLETON.

PRICE 1/1½ Per Bottle.

DEATH OF THE QUEEN - A PEACEFUL ENDING

It is with profound sorrow that we announce the death of Her Majesty the Queen, which took place at Osborne at half-past six o'clock on Tuesday evening. At a few minutes past seven the official bulletin announcing the melancholy news was posted at Osborne House as follows:-

"Osborne, January 22nd, 1901, 6.45pm. Her Majesty the Queen breathed her last at 6.30pm, surrounded by her children and grandchildren.

Signed James Reid M.D.
R Douglas Powell M.D.
Thomas Barlow M.D."

(Salford Reporter 26 January 1901)

SPECIAL NOTICE

Clients will please note
that for their convenience our
NEW OFFICES
136 and 138 CHAPEL STREET,
are now connected with the
NEW TELEPHONE, No. 830.

By this means of communication we trust that our numerous customers will be saved considerable trouble in the matter of correspondence, etc.

THE SALFORD PRINTING COMPANY LIMITED,
136 and 138, CHAPEL STREET, SALFORD
NEW TELEPHONE, No 830
Telegraphic address: Chronicle, Salford

(Salford Chronicle 12 January 1895)

WHOLESALE.

AN AMUSING NOVELTY — The Tango Punch Talk and Whistle 4s. 6d. gross.
SCOUT WHISTLES — 3s. 6d. gross.

CHAPMAN'S, PICTURE FRAMERS,
ST. STEPHEN STREET, SALFORD.

WARNING TO CHILDREN

(Letter to O Duthie, Es., Clerk to the Salford School Board.)

My Dear Sir, I beg to inform you that the Corporation will very shortly commence to run the electric cars in the Borough of Salford and as the danger to be apprehended, particularly to children, from the electric cars is much greater than from the horse cars, owing to their increased speed, I should feel extremely obliged if you would be good enough to request the teachers in your various schools to kindly impress this fact upon the children under their charge, and to particularly warn them against the following practices, which are very prevalent amongst children, viz: Jumping on the cars, placing pins or other articles on the lines in front of the approaching cars, and waiting about at the rear of the cars for tickets, etc.

Yours faithfully, ERNEST HATTON
General Manager, Corporation Tramways Offices

(Salford Reporter 28th September 1901)

ALARMING CARRIAGE ACCIDENT

On Wednesday afternoon an alarming carriage accident took place in Eccles Old Road, Pendleton. A brougham drawn by two horses and which contained Mrs Lightbown of Weaste Hall, Pendleton, Mrs Sugden, Sandy-lane, and Mrs Goulden, of Hazeldene (daughter) was being driven along the road by a coachman named Thomas Norbury, at about 3 o'clock, and when near Summer Hill gate the animal on the off-side threw its leg over one of the traces, with the result that both horses became restive and ultimately dashed off at a great pace. When about 70 yards had been covered the coachman, Norbury, placed the reins round the back of the driver's box and seizing them lower down made a great effort to check the horses' speed. Unfortunately, however, one of the reins broke and the driver, therefore, lost control of the animals, which continued on their career. Shortly afterwards the two near wheels of the brougham passed over a heap of gravel and cement, which is being used in connection with the laying of the new electric tramway, with the result that the coachman lost his seat and fell in the roadway. One of the wheels of the brougham passed over his legs, but fortunately without inflicting any serious injuries. On the way the carriage collided with a watchman's fire and some casks of petroleum, with the result that a hut belonging to Messrs George Hill and Company, Trafford Park, electrical engineers, was set on fire. Information was promptly given to the Salford Fire Brigade and the Pendleton detatchment attended and extinguished the fire. The horses meanwhile continued their gallop, and when opposite Weaste Lane they collided with a pony cart belonging to and driven by Walter Thomas, Alexandra Road, Patricroft, breaking the shafts and slightly injuring the owner. At Broome House the horses were stopped, but not before they had run into a lurry driven by Robert Friars, Silk-street, Eccles, who was also slightly hurt. The occupants of the carriage were naturally much distressed and frightened at their narrow escape. They were immediately taken to an adjoining house and a cab was procured and they were driven to Weaste Hall, and were attended by Dr Worley, who found the ladies suffering from shock. Mrs Lightbown also had a sprained wrist, Mrs Sugden a sprained ankle, but Mrs Goulden was fortunate to escape without injury.

(Salford Reporter March 15 1902)

CAB v MOTORCAR

As part of its endeavours to arrive at a judicious decision in regard to the regulation of motor-cars, the French extra-Parliamentary Commission on Automobiles has held a series of comparative tests for the stopping of cabs and motor-cars. The trial was made in the Bois de Boulogne. The macadam road was very greasy, and the shoes of the horses were quite able to obtain a better grip than the tyres of the cars, which, nevertheless, scored a complere triumph. Two single-horse cabs, one pair-horse coupe, and a pony trap competed against a 6 h.p. light car and a 40 h.p. car weighing nearly 30cwt. At 7½ miles an hour the ordinary cab stopped in 30ft, both cars in 10 ft. At ten miles per hour the best of several attempts showed that the single horse cab came to a standstill in 40ft, and the cars in 13ft. At twelve miles an hour a pair-horse coupe covered 43ft before stopping, while the cars pulled up in 17ft. Following this, as one of the horses, in endeavouring to stop, had badly strained a thigh muscle, the cars alone made one or two tests. At sixteen miles an hour they pulled up in 34ft, at twenty four miles an hour in 60ft. On a dry road the results would be still further in favour of the motor car. The conclusion is that horses are very inefficiently braked.

(Salford Chronicle 12 December 1903)

A LIST OF "DONT'S" WHICH WOMEN SHOULD OBEY

Don't bathe the face while it is very warm or very cold.
Don't bathe in hard water. Soften it with a little powdered borax or a handful of oatmeal.
Don't attempt to remove dust with cold water.
Give the face a hot bath with soap and then rinse thoroughly with clear tepid or cold water.
Don't eat when tired and don't work when tired. It is a mistake to work when not in fit condition - bad for the work and bad for you.
Don't give unnecessary time to a certain established routine of house-work when it could be much more profitably spent in rest and recreation.
Don't forget that the nurses of a woman's beauty are seven:- fresh air, sunshine, warmth, rest, sleep, food, and whatever stirs the blood, be it exercise or enthusiasm.
Don't miss your "beauty sleep", it is a mistake to go to bed too late at night, rise at daybreak, and imagine that every hour taken from sleep is an hour gained.

(Salford Chronicle 5 December 1903)

MASSAGE AND THE COLD TUB

Every knight of the bath should massage himself before getting up and going into the invigourating tub. Just throw your blanket over your head and begin at the toes, and going upwards with the fingers, and rubbing in the same direction - always towards the heart - give yourself a good rough handling. Grip and squeeze and rub and roll every muscle or group of muscles you can get your hands upon all over the body. Work systematically until you are well warmed. Then still with the clcthes over your head rest for three minutes, and after that spring out of bed and seize your big sponge. Squat beside the tub or sitz bath and well lave face, eyes and head. then pop in bodily and after sponging the legs a few times, empty the sponge time after time first over one shoulder and spine, then over the other shoulder and spine, I do not mean you have two spines - do not make me laugh - please, it is the same old spine that catches it whichever shoulder you are engaged in sponging. Mind, the sponge ought to be as big as possible. Two minutes or less will be enough this weather, and in very cold weather one minute. But do not count time, only the

SALFORD BATTALIONS.

THERE'S A VACANT PLACE FOR YOU IN THE SALFORD SECOND BATTALION.

Lord Kitchener has obtained 900,000 recruits, and only 100,000 are needed to make up the first million.

YOU can ENLIST with YOUR PALS at the Pendleton Town Hall.

INSPECTION BY COLONEL TUDWAY.

Salford, it is hoped, will soon be represented in Lord Kitchener's Army by two distinctly local battalions. The First Battalion was completed over a fortnight ago and it is rapidly advancing in efficiency. Last week the committee, of which Mr. C. A. Montague Barlow, M.P., is chairman, decided to undertake the raising of a Second Battalion, and formal leave has been granted to Mr. Barlow by the War Office to raise a new battalion for Salford. Recruiting for this purpose has been going on steadily during the last few days, and up to Thursday 220 recruits were enrolled. The erection of the huts for the camp at Conway is being rapidly proceeded with and contracts are being placed for the construction of a camp for the Second Battalion alongside the first. Mr. Barlow has received a telegram from Lord Kitchener congratulating him and the committee on their success in raising the First Battalion and expressing the hope that Salford would continue to send forward more recruits to meet the country's urgent call. The training of the men is proceeding with very satisfactory results and the enthusiasm with which they have taken up their new calling is evident to all who have seen them passing through the streets on their route marches. On one occasion last week one of the companies marched sixteen miles without a single man falling out. A and B Companies have now received rifles for drilling purposes and about six hundred uniforms of blue serge, with caps of the regulation pattern, have been received, although the majority have yet to be served out. The First Battalion was inspected yesterday (Friday) by Colonel Tudway from Preston. The inspecting officer, accompanied by Colonel Moss (the officer in command of the battalion), Mr. C. A. M. Barlow, M.P., Major Abercrombie (adjutant), Major C. V. Godfrey, Captain Stone and Sergeant-Major Dunne, proceeded to the Castle Irwell Racecourse, where A and D Companies were inspected. There were about 530 men on parade in charge of the following officers—A Company, Lieutenants H. Hartland, R. E. McLeod, L. S. Beyts, and W. B. Armitage; D. Company, Major C. V. Godfrey, Lieutenants MacLaren, L. C. Mandleberg, E. Hampson, Sutcliffe and H.F. Robinson. The men were put through numerous evolutions, and the smartness with which they responded to the word of command, and their precision in marching showed that they are getting the fullest advantage from their training. In turn they were put through company, platoon and section drill and extended order drill and they went through the movements with an alertness and intelligence which not only showed the good use they are making of their instruction, but physical aptitude in a marked degree. At the further end of the racecourse a small detachment under Lieutenant C. F. Harwood went through musketry and skirmishing drill. Colonel Tudway next visited the Broughton drill-ground by the Broughton Town Hall, where he inspected B Company. There were about 250 men on parade and the officers were Lieutenants R. A. Thomas, G. A. Howe, G. Y. Heald and C. H. Wright. The men there were put through the various drill movements and at the close the Inspecting Officer spent some time in personally instructing the section commanders. Afterwards C. Company was inspected at the Lewis Recreation Ground, where the officers in charge were Lieutenants W. Sharratt, R. J. Smith and W. Lowe. The inspecting officer was very favourably impressed with the appearance of the men and the manner in which they executed the different movements. After witnessing two of the companies marching in the close order he turned to Colonel Moss and asked how long they had been in training. When he was informed that they commenced on September 14 he remarked that it was wonderful. He had much praise for the section commanders and said he was very pleased to find so many old soldiers as non-commissioned officers and section leaders. He also expressed satisfaction to Colonel Moss at the keenness of the young O.T.C. officers in the battalion.

RECRUITING MEETING AT ECCLES.

On Saturday afternoon last a strong detachment of the First Salford Battalion marched to Eccles. The object of the visit was to give a stimulus to recruiting for the new Salford Battalion. A number of the men were in uniform, and they presented a smart appearance. It seemed a pity, however, that there was no band of any description to accompany the battalion, and much dissatisfaction was expressed. Major Abercrombie (Adjutant) was in charge, and Mr. C. A. M. Barlow, M.P., was also present. They proceeded to the ground of the Eccles Borough Football Cub who were playing Northwich Victoria. There was a brass band here, and at half time they played the soldiers round the ground to the strains of the "Tipperary" march. The men marched in splendid style and they had a fine reception. At the close of the game, which by the way, was lost by the "Oakemen" by one goal to nil, speeches were delivered from the grand stand by Mr. Barlow and Major Abercrombie. Mr. Barlow said they had recently completed the First Salford Battalion, and he had that morning received a telegram from Lord Kitchener expressing pleasure at the success of their efforts, and pointing out that he was sure Salford would continue to send a steadily supply of men for their country in the national crisis. So, continued, Mr. Barlow, they had decided to form a Second Battalion, and it had been suggested that Eccles should form a "Pals" Company in connection with it. The "Pals" would drill together, go to camp in North Wales together, and finally would together take their places in the trenches side by side with the other gallant members of the British Army— (cheers). Mr. Barlow went on to explain the arrangements he had made in connection with the camp at Conway, and said there was a suitable rifle range in close proximity. They hoped to move into the camp by the end of November. — Major Abercrombie said it was absolutely necessary if they were to push the Germans back that they must have a strong Army. Salford and Eccles had already done well, but more men were wanted. — On the motion of Councillor Anderton, seconded by Mr. A. F. Butterworth, a vote of thanks was passed to the Borough Football Club for the use of the ground for recruiting purposes. — Headed by the band playing the "Marseillaise" the Battalion marched to a plot of ground near the Eccles New Town Hall, where the Eccles Volunteer Athletic Force were on parade. The "Athletes," who are a complete battalion, presented a smart appearance, and they were addressed by Mr. Barlow, M.P., and Major Abercrombie — Mr. Barlow said he desired to congratulate them upon their efforts in forming such a fine battalion for home defence. Still they must not lose sight of the fact that this great battle would not be won in this country but on the plains of France. They must have more men in Lord Kitchener's Army and he would suggest, as he had mentioned at a previous meeting, that they should form an Eccles "Pals" Company in the new Salford Battalion. — The Salford soldiers afterwards marched back to the Pendleton Town Hall, where they were dismissed.

spongefuls, say three over each shoulder. Then out you come, and use two towels with vim and vigour.

(Salford Reporter 26 March 1910)

SALFORD BATTALION

LORD KITCHENER'S ARMY.

Hon. Colonel, Right Hon. the EARL OF DERBY, K.G.

President, The MAYOR OF SALFORD.

Chairman of Committee, Mr. C. A. M. BARLOW, M.P.

LEAVE HAS BEEN GRANTED BY THE WAR OFFICE TO FORM A

Salford Battalion

IN LORD KITCHENER'S ARMY, PROVIDED THE NECESSARY NUMBER, VIZ.:

1,100 ARE ENROLLED.

WHEN THE BATTALION IS FORMED RECRUITS WILL BE ENTITLED TO FULL PAY OF 1s. A DAY, FROM THE DATE OF ATTESTATION.

DURING FORMATION THE BATTALION WILL BE EQUIPPED AND WILL DRILL IN SALFORD, AND RECRUITS WILL BE ABLE TO SLEEP AT HOME, RECEIVING AN ALLOWANCE IN PLACE OF RATIONS AT THE ARMY RATE, WHICH IS AT PRESENT 2s. A DAY. THIS IS IN ADDITION TO THE PAYMENT OF 1s. A DAY.

RECRUITS MUST STATE CLEARLY IF THEY WISH TO ENLIST FOR THE

SALFORD BATTALION.

RECRUITING STATION—

PENDLETON TOWN HALL.

Tel. No. 205 Hr. B'ton. Estab. 1867.

J. E. KIRKHAM,
FUNERAL DIRECTOR & FURNISHER.
15, LOWER BROUGHTON-RD., B'TON.
2, LEICESTER ROAD.

Higher Broughton. Cremations Arranged. Sanitary Oak and Lead Shells on the Shortest Notice.

ANIMAL CAPERS

A tramcar ran into a flock of sheep being driven along Cross-lane, Salford, early on Tuesday morning and killed one.

An unusual incident was witnessed by many people in Cross-lane, Salford, on Tuesday afternoon. One of a herd of cows jumped on the bonnet of a motor van, breaking one of the headlights and a wooden panel on the off side of the windscreen.

(Salford City Reporter 24 November 1923)

POWER OF PUBLICITY

It is not often that one gets such a striking example of the power of publicity as that of the full-page advertisement published in our issue last week for Mr Montague Burton. The shop has been crowded every day this week by men eager to secure the bargains offered of Men's Suits to measure at 37s 6d, and Men's Overcoats at 27s 6d. Of course, these offers are unique and really remarkable achievements, even for Mr Montague Burton, but a great portion of the public would not have known anything about this Magnet Sale if it were not for the enterprising publicity methods adapted by that progressive firm.

(Salford City Reporter 15 December 1923)

BARE LEGS IN THE BALLROOM

There was quite a little commotion in a famous ballroom this week, when three well-known society girls appeared in golden sandals and no stockings. Almost immediately a certain lady, who is trying hard to climb the ladder to fame, disappeared and on returning shortly was seen to have bare legs in place of black silk stockings; as she unfortunately was wearing a black frock and black shoes, her appearance was the cause of mirth, none the less so as her proclivities are now generally recognised.

(Salford City Reporter 24 November 1923)

MORE MOTOR BUSES

The green headlights which have recently been placed on the Salford motorbuses running at night are undoubtedly most useful. It was formerly none too easy to pick out of the ordinary traffic an approaching 'bus which one desired to board, but the innovation has removed that difficulty. The light, which is fixed on top of the front of the omnibus is visible from a considerable distance. Salford is the first town in the country to adopt this method of distinguishing their buses.

(Salford City Reporter 1 December 1923)

LATEST METHOD OF POSTING

On Monday for the first time, letter boxes were placed on seven Salford cars for the receipt of correspondence, under arrangements made with the Tramways Committee and the postal authorities. The letter box, which is of postal red and some twelve inches square and eighteen inches deep, was placed behind the driver's seat in such a way that letters could be put in the box without disturbing the driver. The box was received at the Tramways Office, Pendleton, at 8.27, and the first letter was posted at Swinton by an old gentleman who was very keen to be the first to take advantage of the new service. Assured that his would be the first letter to enter the box, he departed delighted. Two other letters were received before the Pendleton terminus was reached.

Here a young lady tripped from the footpath to the box with a delicately tinted, highly perfumed missive, which she dropped into the box, with a sweet smile. At St Thomas's Church, Pendleton, there was a rush of four men from the footpath, but they had no letters to post. They were simply actuated by curiosity. To the end of the journey the postal-box remained untouched.

At Deansgate it was met by a couple of postmen and a postal official, the former to collect the letters, and the latter to see how the service was likely to work. There was plenty of time to spare, and letters handed over in Pendlebury at nine o'clock would be delivered the following morning.

(Salford City Reporter 10 November 1923)

MODES OF THE MOMENT AND THINGS FEMININE

The newest fad is the walking-stick umbrella, that is, the umbrella that doubles into a walking stick, which is either plain or carved. Handbags are of painted leather, with artistic tops of burnt ivory tone, or of beautiful embroideries mounted in porcelain or its imitation. The two new colours for walking shoes are deep currant red and jade green. Mauve and violet are also seen in walking shoes and any one of the colours named look well against the navy-blue costume or coat-frock.

(Salford City Reporter 27 October 1923)

. ALL .
KODAK
SUPPLIES

films, plates, papers, printing frames, dark room lamps
and all other accessories
at
REDUCED PRICES.

At your service for
PRINTING
Developing
Enlarging
Quick Service · Best Results

NEEDHAM'S
(late HADFIELDS)
PHOTOGRAPHIC CHEMISTS,
116a, LOWER BROUGHTON ROAD

SALFORD'S WAR ON RATS

"Rat Week" in Salford, which began on Monday, is being taken up with enthusiasm, and already Mr Hamblett, the superintendant of the Salford Lighting and Cleansing Department, and rat executive officer for Salford, has received and is receiving enquiries as to adequate measures, both in the way of prevention and cure, for ridding premises of rats and mice. One important point to be borne in mind is that if a block of premises is affected the different occupiers are required to take concerted action. A great many posters are being displayed on the hoardings and in tram-cars to remind the general public of its responsibility, and asking that every effort be made to exterminate the vermin.

(Salford City Reporter 10 November 1923)

Demobilised Men
AND OTHERS
will secure the Best Value to-day — as always — in a
Hepworth Suit
TAILORED-TO-ORDER OR READY-FOR-SERVICE
Remember — when we say Value we mean that we give in addition to First-class workmanship, the Very Best Materials that can be bought for the money
Will you call and see our New Patterns?
HEPWORTHS
THE CLOTHIERS
111 & 111a, BROAD STREET, PENDLETON,
400 & 402, REGENT ROAD, SALFORD.
All Saints, Ardwick, Hr. Openshaw and over 160 Other Branches.

The extracts in this book form part of the extensive collection of local history material held by the Salford Local History Library in Peel Park, Salford

HOURS OF OPENING

Monday	9.00am-5.00pm
Tuesday	9.00am-7.00pm
Wednesday	9.00am-5.00pm
Thursday	9.00am-5.00pm
Friday	9.00am-7.00pm
Saturday	9.00am-1.00pm

We are continually trying to expand the collection and would welcome the donation of old photographs, postcards, newspapers, scrapbooks, bill-heads, church magazines, posters, letters, diaries and other items. (Originals can be copied and returned) If you have anything of interest please let us know.

The Salford Local History Library
Peel Park, Salford M5 4WU Tel. 736 3353

IF YOU ARE INTERESTED IN THE HISTORY OF OUR CITY, WHY NOT PAY US A VISIT?

DANCING.
MISS IDA HILL.
Private Lessons in all the New Dances.
44, THE CRESCENT, SALFORD.

ROBERTSON'S

(OF OLDHAM ST., MANCHESTER)
105 & 107, BROAD STREET, PENDLETON,
198 & 200, REGENT ROAD SALFORD,
31 CHURCH STREET, ECCLES.

GREAT . . .

Money Saving Opportunities
...for Gentlemen This Week...

GENT'S FLANNEL SHIRTS (Lined) **6/11½,** worth 10/11.
GENT'S FLANNEL SHIRTS (Unlined) **5/11½** worth 8/11.
Nice Clean Designs — Splendid Wearing Flannel.

		Former price
Gent's strong Grandrill Shirts	**3/11½**	5/11½
Gent's strong Grandrill Shirts	**4/11½**	6/11
		worth
Gent's strong Grandrill Shirts	**7/11½**	10/11
Gent's Flannelette Shirts	**3/11½**	5/11½
,, ,, ,, ...	**4/11½**	6/11½
Boys' ,, ,, all sizes from	**2/11½**	
Boys' Grandrill Shirts, all sizes from	**2/11½**	
		Out-sizes
Gent's Merino VESTS	**3/11½**	4/11½
		worth
,, All Wool ,, ...	**6/11½**	10/11
,, Shetland ,, ...	**4/11½**	8/11½
		Usual price
,, All Wool Shetland Vests	**6/11**	10/11

PANTS to Match all Above, **SAME PRICE.**

GENT'S all Wool Ribbed SOCKS **1/- pair,** usual price 1/11½.

Gent's All Wool Cashmere Socks **1/6½ pair,** worth 2/6.

Gent's All Wool Ribbed Socks **1/6½ pair,** worth 2/11½.

Gent's All Wool Embroidered Socks, **2/11½ p'r,** worth 3/11½.

ENGINEERS' OVERALLS, Bib and Brace, Indigo and Brown, **4/11½,** worth 8/11½.
Painters' Strong Jackets with 3 Pockets, **4/11½,** former price 8/11½.

Our Policy has always been to give sound value at the lowest possible price. By sound value we do not mean just what we can get for an article, or even what it is worth, because in the first place the article must be worth wearing and must wear well. Having satisfied ourselves that the article is worth wearing, and is of good quality we fix a keen price and offer it to the public with every assurance that it will give satisfaction.

SPECIAL PURCHASE: Gent's Knitted Ties **1/- each,** usual price 1/11½.
Gent's Silk Wide-end Ties **1/11½ each** usual prices 2/11½ and 3/11½

These are lovely ties, all good designs and will make most acceptable Gifts for Xmas, Gifts that will be appreciated by Gentlemen.

ROBERTSON'S, *The Keen Price Drapers.*
BRANCHES EVERYWHERE.

PAINLESS DENTISTRY.
TEETH. Single Tooth from 2s.6d.
TEETH. Set from 21s.
TEETH. Painless Extractions with Gas, Cocaine, Etc.

Littlewood,
DENTAL SURGERY,
549, LIVERPOOL STREET, WEST, SEEDLEY.

ENGLISH AND AMERICAN DENTISTRY.
G. SCHOLES
70, BROAD STREET, PENDLETON; also at 133 and 135, STATION ROAD, Pendlebury.

Attendance at own residence by appointment. All communications should be addressed to the Head Surgery at PENDLETON.

MODERN DENTISTRY.
Consult MR. O. HANSON.
Hours, 9 a.m. to 7 30 p.m. Sats. 9 to 6.
ESTABLISHED 1909.
8, HOWARD STREET, ECCLES NEW ROAD, SALFORD (Near Salford Union).

DENTISTRY.
JAS. JOHNSTON,
377, BOLTON ROAD,
IRLAMS-O'TH'-HEIGHT,
(Opposite the Post Office).

SPEND YOUR CHECK
In the Cheapest Shop in the District.
FOR GLASS AND CHINA :: ::
:: :: FOR CARPETS and OILCLOTHS.
Agent Wanted for Nic-Nac Clubs.
LOUIS ZIMMERMAN,
123, ELLOR STREET, PENDLETON.

Established 1882.
H. J. WHEATLEY,
Family Butcher, VICTORIA BRIDGE, SALFORD, Manchester. Tel. 2264 City.
Corned Beef and Pickled Tongues.
Beef and Pork Sausages (our own make).
MINCED BEEF.
Ground Bone, the best food for Poultry.

FALCON INN,
CROSS LANE, (Corner of Hodge Lane),
Wilson's Noted ALES and STOUT in fine condition.
Cigars and cigarettes of all Choicest Brands.
D. ALLARDYCE, PROPRIETOR

JOSEPH HEMINGWAY (Associate),
Pianist and Organist.
Teacher of Pianoforte, Organ, Harmony, Theory, etc.
Gives Lessons and Has Vacancies for Pupils.
Pupils successful at Musical Examinations.
Special attention to tone production in Pianoforte Playing. PUPILS VISITED.
Fees by Arrangement.
131, CHURCH-ST., and 77, SEAFORD-ROAD PENDLETON.

MARSH'S ACADEMY,
323, BROAD STREET, PENDLETON.
SHORTHAND, TYPING, BOOKKEEPING, BUSINESS ROUTINE, FRENCH, etc.

OPEN DAILY. 9-30 a.m. to 9-30 p.m.

MISS CUNDALL, A.I.U.M., Gold Medallist, L.G.M.T., Teacher of the Pianoforte, 148, Broad Street, PENDLETON. — Pupils prepared for

---

MUSICAL INSTRUMENTS OF EVERY DESCRIPTION,
At PRICES to SUIT EVERYBODY.
First Class Teachers for all Instruments.
H. EMMET
15, BROAD STREET, PENDLETON

****

For a current list of local history publications available by post, please send a stamped addressed envelope to Neil Richardson, 88 Ringley Road, Stoneclough, Radcliffe, Manchester M26 9ET

****